GREAT LEADERS

MAKE SURE

MONDAY MORNING

DOESN'T SUCK

GREAT LEADERS

MAKE SURE

MONDAY MORNING
DOESN'T SUCK

HOW TO GET, KEEP & GROW TALENT

ERIC HARKINS

ForbesBooks

Published by ForbesBooks, Charleston, South Carolina.
Member of Advantage Media Group.

ForbesBooks is a registered trademark, and the ForbesBooks colophon is a trademark of Forbes Media, LLC.

Printed in the United States of America.

10 9 8 7 6 5 4 3 2

ISBN: 978-1-950863-83-9
LCCN: 2021912504

This custom publication is intended to provide accurate information and the opinions of the author in regard to the subject matter covered. It is sold with the understanding that the publisher, Advantage|ForbesBooks, is not engaged in rendering legal, financial, or professional services of any kind. If legal advice or other expert assistance is required, the reader is advised to seek the services of a competent professional.

 Advantage Media Group is proud to be a part of the Tree Neutral® program. Tree Neutral offsets the number of trees consumed in the production and printing of this book by taking proactive steps such as planting trees in direct proportion to the number of trees used to print books. To learn more about Tree Neutral, please visit **www.treeneutral.com.**

Since 1917, Forbes has remained steadfast in its mission to serve as the defining voice of entrepreneurial capitalism. ForbesBooks, launched in 2016 through a partnership with Advantage Media Group, furthers that aim by helping business and thought leaders bring their stories, passion, and knowledge to the forefront in custom books. Opinions expressed by ForbesBooks authors are their own. To be considered for publication, please visit **www.forbesbooks.com.**

DEDICATION

This book is dedicated to my niece, Shannon Anne O'Hara. Shannon was diagnosed with DIPG, an inoperable brain tumor, on April 15, 2011. She died on January 6, 2012—less than nine months later. She was thirteen years old.

Do what makes you happy.

It's probably the best lesson I learned from Shannon. In her thirteen short years, she lived life to the fullest. When she was receiving daily chemotherapy and radiation treatments, she scheduled her appointments over the lunch hour so she could still go to school and be with her friends. She still played golf. She still played hockey. She still hung out with her friends because all those things made her happy.

She had one of the most positive, upbeat personalities of anyone I've ever met—and she was facing death as a young teenager.

Life isn't fair, and everyone knows it. You have to play the hand you're dealt. The good news for most people reading this is that you can change your hand. Shannon never got the chance. You can go all in, or you can fold. You choose. Do what makes you happy, and the things you spend most of your time worrying about won't seem so important anymore.

CONTENTS

CHAPTER ONE
SETTING THE STAGE

In my last corporate role, I was the chief administrative officer for a $1.5B retail company. We shared an office with a bank. One morning, I got on the elevator with two of their employees.

Their exchange made me sigh a little:

Him: "Good morning."
Her: "Good morning."
Him: "How was your weekend?"
Her: "Good. How are you doing?"
Him: "Good. Except that it's Monday."
Her: "Yeah, except that it's Monday."

How many people do you know who get a sick feeling in their stomach on Sunday night just thinking about going to work? They show up first thing on Monday morning and they're already in a bad mood.

Your only job as a leader is to make sure Monday morning doesn't suck.

Yep, it's that simple. If you lead people, you are there to create a culture high performers want to be part of. If you have employees driving to work on Monday morning with that sick feeling in their stomach, you can fix that. It's probably because they are high performers, but you haven't told them that. Or they are low performers, but you haven't told them that. Or they are stuck in the middle, and you haven't given them any direction.

I hope if you ask high performers who have worked for me if I was a good boss, they would say something like "He was a good boss," or "I really liked working for him," or "I'd work for him again," or something like that. I suspect if you asked low performers who worked for me if I was a good boss, they'd say something like, "Yeah, I didn't really like him that much."

YOUR ONLY JOB AS A LEADER IS TO MAKE SURE MONDAY MORNING DOESN'T SUCK.

I am okay with both. I don't think that's arrogance; I think it's leadership. You have to be okay with both. And you have to accept that it is your responsibility as a leader to know that some people will make it and others won't. My job as a leader is, was, and will always be to create a culture that high-performing people want to be a part of. High-performing. You shouldn't care if low-performing employees or people who quit but haven't given you their notice think you're a good boss. Focus on the high performers and create a culture they want to be a part of.

■　■　■

A little bit of my story … I've had quite the journey. My career started in 1995 at Target Corporation. My first position was ETL (executive team leader), which meant assistant store manager. Over the course of my career, I ended up working in operations, sales, and human resources, mostly in retail and mainly in HR.

I was lucky to be a head of HR three times. I've worked for companies that were Fortune 500, Fortune 100, Fortune 50, publicly traded, privately held, family owned, private equity owned, and consulting based in the retail, healthcare, business-to-business, consumer packaged goods, technology, and career transition services industries.

I've been a manager, director, vice president, executive vice president, president, chief human resources officer, and chief administrative officer.

This crazy journey has given me experiences that shaped how I showed up as a leader and what I think it takes to have a company that people really want to work for.

In other words, I learned how to make sure Monday morning doesn't suck.

It's not that hard. Most companies just aren't willing to do what it takes to hold every leader accountable to this one simple goal—create a company people genuinely love working for.

I was lucky enough to be part of a company that did that. I was even luckier to work for a lot of companies that didn't.

This book is a compilation of stories, management philosophies, and leadership principles built from twenty-five years of working my way up the corporate ladder. I've worked for a lot of companies. I've worked for a lot of leaders. I've done a lot of things right and I've done a lot of things wrong. And I learned a lot of things along the way …

I hope you enjoy reading this book as much as I enjoyed writing it.

CHAPTER TWO
GOOD LEADERS LEAD

The higher your level, the less you should know. Well, that might not be exactly true, but I do believe that the higher your level, the less of a subject matter expert you need to be.

I was interviewing to be the head of HR at a large chain of restaurants in the sports bar category. The company did about $500M in revenue at the time and was growing fast. I was really excited about the opportunity, as I loved everything they stood for. It was down to two candidates—me and another guy.

The other guy got it.

I always considered that opportunity the one that got away. I think about it every time I eat there. They are over $2B in revenue now. I had met with most of the executive team and passed. I had met with the CEO and passed. I had met a few people from HR and passed. One more interview to go and an offer would be coming.

The one more interview was with their CFO. The one more interview did not go well.

At one point during the interview, the CFO asked me, "If needed in a pinch, would you be able to run payroll?"

I said, "Absolutely not."

She said, "Really?"

I told her I didn't know how to run payroll, but I did know how to hire people who know how to run payroll.

Apparently, that was not the answer she was looking for. When I found out that the other guy got the job and then found out who the other guy was, I was certain he would be able to run payroll if needed in a pinch. And that doesn't mean he's bad. I've met him and had lunch with him. He's a really good guy and helped build that company for years.

As my career began at Target Corporation, I was lucky because I worked there when Bob Ulrich led the company. He was a great CEO.

Bob came up with a new idea: instead of promoting the obvious choice for the next big job, promote the next in line after the obvious choice, the up-and-comer who probably has more long-term potential. This was incredibly controversial within the company—and incredibly successful. Bob got way more promotions right than wrong.

What it taught me was that you don't need to know how to do everything in your "function" if you lead a team. You really don't. I'd actually argue you shouldn't. What you need to accept is the fact that being a great leader means hiring people who are way smarter than you to run the function for you. You're simply there to make the lives of your team easier. If the head of a department in your company is making all the decisions, you might have bigger issues to acknowledge, and I'd start paying attention to the engagement of your high-potential people.

Even though I have been head of HR at three companies, I don't know that much about HR. I'm not being funny. I really don't. I guarantee I couldn't pass an SHRM certification. Every now and then a friend or family member will call me with an HR question. I rarely know the answer. But I could always get them the answer. I just had to ask someone on my team.

I might not know much about HR, but let me tell you what I did learn a lot about during my journey:

- Creating a culture high performers want to be a part of

- Making sure Monday morning doesn't suck

Through the years, I started to write down things I saw really good leaders do. Consistently. Every day. Not because they were told to but because they were leaders who were genuinely passionate about leading people. I call this collection of great leadership traits LEAD:

IT'S OKAY TO HAVE FUN AT WORK.

LEAD

LEADERSHIP EXPECTATIONS AND DEVELOPMENT

- Create a culture high performers want to be a part of

- Bring energy and enthusiasm to work every day

- Build relationships at all levels of the organization

- Support the direction of the company—no hidden agendas

- Be decisive—make the tough call when it needs to be made

- Manage the performance of your team(s)

- Consistently deliver results

- Help the company grow by developing people

You have to have something like LEAD in your company. You have to. This is the most important tool I use when I work with leaders. I will discuss this throughout the book, but you cannot create a company where Monday morning doesn't suck if you don't have great leaders. As simple as it sounds, the questions are "Do your leaders know what's expected of them?" and "Do they know how they need to show up each day?" That's different from understanding what their job is.

I want you to think about leaders you have in your company. Are they the subject matter experts in their function? I bet a lot of them are. Do they make most of the decisions in their area because they know more than the people who work for them? Most likely. Do they develop their teams by learning from them and empowering their people to run their areas without needing much guidance? Hopefully, but if not, you can fix that.

Subject matter experts like being subject matter experts. And given the opportunity, they will do what they do best—be subject matter experts.

Good leaders like being good leaders and have less desire to be subject matter experts. They are too busy developing their teams by unleashing their potential and helping them achieve and exceed their goals.

There is a big difference between experts and leaders.

CHAPTER THREE

THREE LESSONS I'VE LEARNED ALONG THE WAY

One benefit of having multiple experiences at multiple companies is the many lessons you learn.

There are three that have shaped my career:

- **Lesson #1:** It's okay to have fun at work.

- **Lesson #2:** Poor performing employees don't quit voluntarily.

- **Lesson #3:** Assholes are assholes. They don't change.

Lesson #1: It's Okay to Have Fun at Work

It really is. It's more than okay to have fun at work. I've been fascinated throughout my career to work with people who don't agree with this. When I worked for a tech company, having fun at work was not a problem. It was a pretty cool environment. Our office was unique, and we would get requests for tours all the time. I loved giving them, not just because I got to show off our awesome employees and cool space, but because of the conversations I'd have after.

I gave a tour once to a group of about twenty leaders from a Fortune 50 company, a very conservative Fortune 50 company with very traditional paradigms among the leadership team. After the tour, the VP of the team, who was trying hard to change the culture in his department, said, "Eric, this is what I want. This is what we need. How do we create *this?*"

I asked him a question. "If your CEO was walking down the hall at 2:00 p.m. on a Tuesday and saw a group of people playing Hacky Sack, how would they react?"

His response was predictable. "They'd be pissed."

And that's why they'd never be able to have fun at work.

Who cares if employees play Hacky Sack on company time? Who cares if they take a nap on the couch? Who cares if they leave in the middle of the day to go to a movie?

Seriously, why do you care?

I know what your answer is: "Because I don't pay them to go to a movie in the middle of the day." No, you pay them to do their job. Are they doing their job? It's a yes or no question. Do they get their work done? That's a yes or no question too. Do they perform at a high level? Do people like working with them? Do they consistently deliver results while bringing energy and enthusiasm to work? Yes or no. If yes, then who cares? If they don't do their job, get rid of them. But if you're going to blame a game of Hacky Sack instead of admitting your leaders might not believe that it's okay to have fun at work, then you have some work to do. I would encourage you to introduce a tool like LEAD.

Lesson #2: Poor Performing Employees Don't Quit Voluntarily

Every team of ten people has at least one person who isn't operating at the level you'd like. It doesn't necessarily mean they need to be fired (though they might), but it does mean they need feedback and direction they probably haven't gotten yet. If you don't address the one person who isn't performing, I promise one of three things will happen to the other nine:

1. Three of them will start modeling the negative behavior because you've let it be acceptable.

2. Three of them will quit and go where they think they have a better chance of being recognized (Note—even if someone isn't a high performer but thinks they are, they will go somewhere else if they think their contributions are not being recognized).

3. And three of them will, unfortunately, quit but never give you notice. You have them in your company right now, because every company does, people who still come to work but "quit" you a long time ago. They show up every day, but they're checked out. They aren't buying what you're selling. They aren't even buying what they're selling. They're doing the minimum possible every day and are doing more harm than you realize.

So what do you do about it?

Unfortunately, poor performing employees don't quit voluntarily. We all wish they did, but they don't. Think about it this way—when was the last time a poor performer came into your office or talked to you on Zoom and quit voluntarily? Now, think about the last time a high performer, someone you didn't want to lose, gave their notice.

Yeah, I know. I hadn't thought of it that way before either.

Being a leader is hard, and most people underestimate the responsibility that comes with having direct reports. It isn't easy. It's draining at times. It can be stressful. But it is especially hard, draining, and stressful when you have poor performers on your team.

We live in a world where too many employees look for a job where they don't have to work too hard, can screw around during the day, come in late, leave early, call in sick all the time, and do the bare minimum.

Having difficult, performance-related conversations is one of the biggest opportunities for almost every leader I've ever worked with. Nobody likes having tough conversations. Most leaders dread the thought of firing someone. I've fired a lot of people throughout my career, and I don't like doing it. I've never gone home and high-fived my wife after I terminated someone (okay, maybe a couple times). But it is part of being a leader, and you can't hide from it. You need to get over it and have the tough conversation. And if you lead a team and can't do that, ask for help. Find a mentor, coach, HR partner or peer who's willing to help you get better at it.

You owe it to your company—and the other nine.

> If you want to make everyone happy, don't become a leader. Sell ice cream.
> ## –STEVE JOBS

Lesson #3: Assholes are Assholes. They Don't Change.

It's true. We are who we are. Sure, we all choose our attitude on any given day, but assholes are assholes.

Why do some people walk by a piece of garbage in the middle of the hall while some people stop, pick it up, and throw it in the trash? Why do some people walk past the receptionist every morning without acknowledging them while others stop each day and ask them how they're doing? Why do some leaders get to know their teams and others don't?

Because we are who we are.

People always ask me, "What's your definition of an asshole?" I tell them I don't know the exact definition, but I know who they are in every company I've ever worked at. Sometimes they are the person I didn't hire because of how they treated people in our office during their interview. Sometimes it's the candidate I didn't hire because my administrative assistant told me how poorly they treated them. And sometimes it's the person who carries the brand of "Oh ... that's just Mark being Mark."

I can't tell you how many times people have used a line like that … and the person, for whatever reason, is let off the hook because "that's just who they are." There is no training or recovery for assholeism. Inpatient or outpatient. Don't try to find it. You can send them to the best leadership training in the world and all you're going to have is the same bad leader and less money in your company's bank account.

You know who they are. You know you do. The second you read Lesson #3, we both know you immediately thought about someone.

Life is too short to work with assholes.

One of my favorite phrases to use with leaders is "If you're not sure, you're sure." It's pretty good life advice. Most of the decisions we make in our lives aren't really that hard because we know the right thing to do even if we don't do it. I think this is really good life advice, but it is great leadership advice. If you're not sure you have the right leader, then you're sure. If you're not sure you should hire that candidate, then you're sure. If you're not sure you should promote that person, then you're sure.

You get the point. It's powerful.

I also like the Golden Rule from kindergarten, a timeless classic. Treat others the way you want to be treated. I've always been fascinated by leaders who treat their direct reports and teams poorly. Fascinated by it. I don't get it.

Now … being honest, direct, firm but fair with someone who isn't performing? That's different. But ignoring someone, setting them up to fail, intentionally creating an environment that's so miserable you hope the person will quit on their own because you don't have the courage to manage their performance? Doing something like sending someone else to fire your direct report? Not cool.

IF YOU'RE NOT SURE, YOU'RE SURE.

CHAPTER FOUR
CARDS AGAINST HUMANITY

Have you ever played Cards Against Humanity? It might be the most inappropriate, R-rated, controversial game ever invented. I absolutely love it.

Best. Game. Ever.

I once hosted an event at my office for a large group of recruiters who worked for a Fortune 50 company. As I was walking around with the leader of the team, she noticed Cards Against Humanity sitting on someone's desk.

I was the chief human resources officer at the time, and we were standing in the HR department. Our exchange went something like this:

Her: "You let people have Cards Against Humanity on their desks?"

Me: "Sure, why not?"

Her: "It's so wrong."

Me: "It's so wrong, it's right."

Her: "You don't let them play it at work, do you?"

Me: "Only if they include me."

Her: "You're kidding."

Me: "Um, it's my favorite game of all time."

Her: "What if someone gets offended?"

Me: "Then they probably shouldn't play."

Her: "I can't believe that."

Me: "Can't believe what?"

Her: "I'd never let people play that at work."

Me: "That's why leaders get frustrated with human resources sometimes."

If I had to sum up in one story what keeps a company from building the type of culture they think they want, there it is. That's why I worked really hard when I was the head of HR to not be a head of HR. I get it; that game isn't for everyone. But if you hire and work with adults, you should treat them like adults. I think the worst thing that happened when my team played Cards Against Humanity together was that some people felt a little queasy afterward because they had been laughing so hard their stomachs hurt.

I'll take that pain at the office every day.

Having a culture that allows things like Cards Against Humanity does not mean harassment, racist jokes, or discrimination are okay. When someone takes advantage of what they perceive to be a "loose" culture, it isn't because you let them play Cards Against Humanity. It's because they are probably an asshole.

When I was interviewing to become head of HR at a tech company in Minneapolis, my first interview was over lunch with the CEO and founder. He started lunch by saying, "Eric, I know we need to hire an HR leader, but I'm scared to do it. We have a unique culture, and my experience with HR people hasn't been great."

I said, "Well, I might not be the right guy to ask because, to be honest, I hate human resources, at least what you think human resources is."

He sat back and said, "Do you think it's possible to be head of HR without being head of HR?"

He had me at hello.

Adults want to be treated like adults. I think a lot of companies, and more specifically a lot of leaders, get caught up in things like Cards Against Humanity because they aren't holding their team accountable. If you walk by someone who's watching a YouTube video at their desk in the middle of the day, it shouldn't matter. Are they getting their work done? Are they a top performer? Do you have to follow up with them constantly? Most leaders react to the game rather than the behavior. Cards, a video, Instagram, Snapchat—those are the games. Your employees are the players. Any high-performing adult should play whatever game they want, whenever and wherever they want, including at the office. *But*—if that same person doesn't bring energy and enthusiasm to work, if they don't execute, if they aren't a top performer, if they quit but haven't given you their notice, then it's a different story. No performance = no Cards Against Humanity.

Don't hate the game. Hate the player.

ADULTS WANT TO BE TREATED LIKE ADULTS.

CHAPTER FIVE

GET. KEEP. GROW.

I came up with this while I was the head of human resources at a family-owned manufacturing company. I was trying to explain "What does HR really do to support the business anyway?" But I've always believed that these are the only three things a company should care about every day: what are we doing to get talent, keep talent, and grow talent? If you're in a leadership role and not spending most of your time thinking about this, then you're wasting a lot of time on stuff that doesn't matter. My longtime mentor, Dan, told me the first time I met him, "Recruiting is the most important part of any organization." Years later, I have come to realize that is true.

Get

How strong is your recruiting team? How confident are you in their ability? Is your best recruiter the best salesperson you have in the company? I hope so. That's all they're doing—selling.

A lot of organizations don't think about the fact that recruiting truly is a sales job. Other than your receptionist (if you have one), recruiters are usually the first point of contact for prospective employees. They set the tone and, whether you believe it or not, they can do just as much damage as good. When you think about the recruiters in your organization, ask yourself these questions: Do you think your recruiters are buying what they are selling? Are they aligned to your company's vision? Do they understand what you're trying to accomplish as an organization? And are they the type of people you'd like to work with every day? If the answer is no, especially to the last question, move on. You're wasting your time with them. Invite them to go to your biggest competitor.

I've always believed that being a recruiter is the easiest position to be a hero in and the quickest one to get fired from.

Keep

Performance management is not a one-time event.

It isn't just an annual review process. It isn't just when someone is not performing. It isn't just when you're so pissed off you can't stand to even look at that person anymore and you just want them gone. Keeping talent is hard. It takes work. It's fluid and should be happening every day through one on ones, coaching, feedback, measurement, and fun. Yes, it includes more formal checkpoints like the initial goal setting when someone is hired or starts a new job, a ninety-day check-in, and the annual review process. One of the biggest mistakes a leader makes is relying on the formal checkpoints to drive retention and engagement rather than making it part of your focus every day in every interaction you have.

Author's note: I promise that the graph I'm about to show is the only time I will reference something that you'd expect to see in a PowerPoint presentation that you're paying BCG or McKinsey a lot of money for. It would probably be buried in a one-hundred-page deck as Slide #88. But it's good, and it's true. And if your leaders believe performance management is not a one-time event and isn't just the annual review process, then you're on the right track.

PERFORMANCE MANAGEMENT IS NOT A ONE-TIME EVENT.

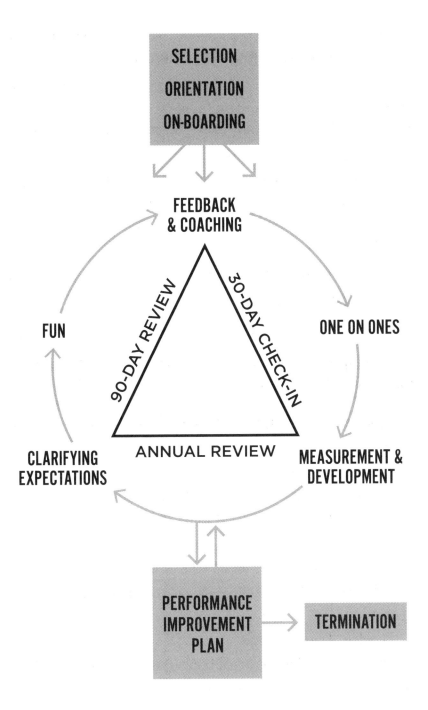

An illustrative guide for leaders—the employee lifecycle.

It starts with the selection process, new hire orientation, and initial training. Are you setting goals with your new hire in their first thirty days? Do they understand what's expected of them on day one, week one, month one? Once they're hired, they go into the "cycle." Leaders should be providing feedback, coaching, learning and development, clarifying expectations, monitoring progress, and having one on ones with their team(s) daily. If you've provided everything in the employee lifecycle and someone isn't performing, they move to a performance improvement plan. At this point, there are only two options:

1. Their performance improves, and they move back into the employee lifecycle.

2. They are terminated.

During my twenty or so years in human resources, I've probably had a hundred conversations that went something like this:

Leader: "I am so frustrated with Johnnie. I want him gone. Today."

Me: "What's the problem?"

Leader: "He is always late. He was late again today. In fact, I bet he's been late ten times in the last three weeks. I want him gone."

Me: "Does he know he needs to be on time?"

Leader: "What do you mean? Of course he does!"

Me: "How many times have you talked to him about being late in the last month?"

Leader: "Umm … none."

Me: "Do you think he might think it's okay since he's always late and nobody has told him that's not acceptable?"

Leader: "So … I can't fire him today then?"

Feedback on a performance review should never be a surprise to an employee, but unfortunately it often is. If you believe that your job as a leader is to make sure Monday morning doesn't suck, then you have to provide all the things in the chart on the previous page. All the time. Every day.

When an employee is not meeting or exceeding the requirements of the job, it's your responsibility as a leader to address it. Right away. Don't wait until your frustration is so high you've lost any interest in giving them a chance to improve their performance.

Another mistake leaders make is defining "performance management" as something you need to do only when someone isn't performing well. I actually think the bigger issue in most companies is that the high performers—the rock stars—don't realize you think they are rock stars.

I've never understood why, but a lot of leaders do not take time to get to know their team, and worse, they don't take the time to let their team get to know them. This should be something you do, not because someone tells you to, but because you genuinely want to get to know your team. If you're faking it, your team will know. If you don't like doing it or don't think it's important as a leader, do your boss a favor and consider stepping down. At least spend some time asking yourself why you want to be a leader. If you have a team and don't have any interest in getting to know the people who work for you at an individual level, ask yourself why. If you can't come up with a good answer, talk to someone who can help you figure it out. Or you could call your boss and tell them you don't want to lead people anymore. It's okay. Not everybody likes it.

When was the last time you did something with your direct reports outside of the office just to have fun and get to know them better? If your answer is something like "I do that every year, right around the holidays," you can do better. One of the things I've found incredibly effective is a GTKM (Get to Know Me) slide. It's simple, not much to it—your life in pictures. I've done this with different teams, and every time I do, I am amazed by the fact that even people who have worked together for years usually don't know that much about each other. It's sad.

It goes something like this: I grew up in Rochester, Minnesota, and went to St. Cloud State University. I've lived in Minnesota, Iowa, Colorado, California, and North Carolina throughout my career. I raised my kids in Shakopee, Minnesota, with my wife Jennifer. We have a twenty-year-old daughter (who goes to college in North Carolina), Laurynn, and seventeen-year-old son, Jack. We're all black belts. There is no such thing as bad pizza. My favorite place on earth is Madeline Island, Wisconsin, but I love Las Vegas too. My favorite author is John Sanford. My first car was a 1982 Chevrolet Chevette I bought from the high school librarian for $300 and totaled ten days later. I am a die-hard Minnesota Vikings fan, soccer was my favorite sport to play growing up, I like to golf, and *Miracle* is my favorite movie.

Pretty simple. Pretty fast. And in ten minutes or less, your team gets to know you in a way that they probably didn't before. You might find common ground. You might find shared interests.

You might actually have fun with your team—imagine what that could feel like.

There's an old saying that people don't quit companies, they quit bosses. I think this is true about 99.9 percent of the time.

Grow

How do you recognize potential in someone? How do you know if they're ready for the next level or more responsibility? It's hard. GE and Target Corporation used versions of the "Es of Excellence" to determine what they looked for in a leader:

Energy + Enthusiasm + Execution = Excellence.

It's short, it's memorable, and it doesn't leave room for a lot of misinterpretation. It is so simple and so accurate.

When you invest in someone, think about the Es of Excellence as the "ease" of excellence. If someone doesn't naturally have energy or enthusiasm, and if they don't consistently execute, they're missing most of what you should look for. I get criticized sometimes when I talk about energy and enthusiasm. I hear things like "not everyone is an excitable person," "Not everyone is as positive as you all the time," or "Not everyone can be running on high all day." I think that's a total cop-out. Energy and enthusiasm aren't about doing cartwheels down the hall or high-fiving everyone you walk by. It's about passion. Believing in what you're doing. Getting your team excited about what's going on. Being real. Making sure Monday morning doesn't suck.

Do you know who your high potentials are? Better yet, do they know you know who they are? Do you have a formal succession planning process? Have you had a meeting with your top executives where you discussed the top talent on their teams and discussed opportunities for them to continue to excel and contribute to your organization? If you said yes, keep doing it. If you said no, start doing it. I had a conversation with a senior-level HR executive several years ago. She was being recruited by Google. Yes, that Google. She was seriously considering quitting, so she talked to her boss. The reaction from her boss and her boss's boss shocked her. She found out very quickly how valued she was. She heard things she had never heard before. She received a phone call from the head of HR for the first time ever. She said no to Google—yes, Google—and decided to stay.

One of the worst things that happens to a high performer is they find out how valued they are about two minutes after giving their notice. Sadly, this happens all the time. If you aren't doing succession planning for your leaders, you should start. There are a lot of tools out there. I like to use a simple template that I've had for over twenty years, which still works.

TALENT REVIEW

High Potential	Highly Valued	Needs Work/ Worth Investment	Problem Performer	Too New To Rate
Name: Title:	Name: Title:	Name: Title:	Name: Title:	Name: Title:
Name: Title:	Name: Title:	Name: Title:	Name: Title:	Name: Title:
Name: Title:	Name: Title:	Name: Title:	Name: Title:	Name: Title:

Not really that complicated. Simply review every manager, director, vice president, and senior executive you have and put them in a category: High Potential, Highly Valued, Needs Work/Worth Investment, Problem Performer, or Too New to Rate (which is typically less than six months).

Every leader in your company should have their backup on their team.

Do you have a culture that gets leaders excited about having their backup, or do they feel threatened? There's a big difference between the two, and I've worked more places where it's the latter than the former. But if your leaders are not A players, I promise they are not excited by the idea of having their own backup on their team. If your leaders have their backup, congratulations. If they don't have their backup, make them get one.

And if they don't and you don't care, you'll likely start losing the nine until you address the one.

ONE OF THE WORST
THINGS THAT HAPPENS
TO A HIGH PERFORMER
IS THEY FIND OUT HOW
VALUED THEY ARE
ABOUT TWO MINUTES
AFTER GIVING THEIR
NOTICE.

CHAPTER SIX

CAN A BAD LEADER CREATE A GOOD CULTURE?

NO.

CHAPTER SEVEN

THE FOUR Cs OF TERMINATION

The best way to reduce turnover in your company is to fire more people. I'll give you a second to think about that.

High-performing people will leave your organization if they have to work with poor performers. Terminating employees is part of being a leader. A players want to work with A players. They just do. And true A players know who the other A players are and, more importantly, who they aren't.

Consider asking every person you interview who's going to lead people if they've ever fired someone—and not because of a policy violation, theft, or something easy like that.

Have you ever fired a person who just wasn't a fit? Who, despite your efforts, just didn't get it? If you have leaders who answer no to that question, you might want to dig a little deeper during the interview. Ask a few more questions about being decisive and making a tough call when a tough call needs to be made. It isn't a fun part of the job, but it is part of the job. You can't hide from terminations. I was head of HR at one company where my boss fired two of his administrative assistants—one was fired on her fifth day, and one was fired in her ninth hour.

Sorry, correction to my last sentence—*I* once fired two of my boss's administrative assistants; he wasn't even in the room. Couldn't do it. He knew they needed to be fired. He knew they were the wrong people for the job. He was the president of the company and too scared to have that conversation.

When I work with leaders preparing to fire someone—especially when it's their first or second time doing it—I ask them to think about the Four Cs of termination:

- **Be CONFIDENT**

  The employee being terminated needs to realize you know you made the right decision.

- **Be CALM**

  Don't let anything change your composure—it's not an emotional event.

- **Be COMMITTED**

  There is no room for negotiation—the decision is final.

- **Be CAUTIOUS**

  Don't answer a question you weren't asked.

If a termination takes more than about two minutes, you've done something wrong. The work, the part that takes a hell of a lot longer than two minutes, is everything you've done leading up to this moment. Clear expectations. Follow-up. Feedback. Coaching. Focusing and refocusing. Making sure they understand the repercussions of not hitting their objectives. The termination is the culmination of weeks if not months of feedback and clarifying that things are not good and that termination is a likely scenario.

People tell me they think it's a little harsh to say two minutes is the maximum length of a termination discussion. Lots of people feel that way. But I believe it's true. The only thing you do by extending a termination discussion is open the door for the employee to feel that there's room for negotiation. This is probably because you didn't follow the Four Cs: You didn't seem confident. You didn't seem committed (worse case: the person doing the terminating blames it on someone else. Oh yeah, that happens. All the time). You weren't calm—you were nervous and scattered. And you weren't cautious—you answered a question you weren't asked.

IF A TERMINATION TAKES MORE THAN ABOUT TWO MINUTES, YOU'VE DONE SOMETHING WRONG.

If you aren't comfortable having the conversation (and honestly … I'm not sure anyone is ever "comfortable"), then read from a script. Really. I coach leaders all the time to write it out and read it. While it might feel a bit cold or impersonal, at least you'll hit the important points, and it's easier to be confident, calm, committed, and cautious if you're simply reading. Be respectful and let them know why. For example, "I have a very difficult and important message to deliver this morning and want to be respectful and make sure I cover the important parts of the message, so I'm going to start by reading from a script." Then when you're done, thank them for their contributions, wish them the best for their future, and end the conversation. You can do all that in two minutes. I promise.

One of the best lessons I learned early in my career during a crisis management training session was to never answer a question you weren't asked. If you're terminating an employee and you're anticipating a question ("What about Sally's performance? It's worse than mine."), don't go there. Don't volunteer something like "I'm sure you're wondering about Sally. We both know her performance isn't great either, and I'm dealing with it." I've had so many conversations with leaders after a termination that required follow-up or left the "termination" conversation with questions that needed to be answered. Why do that? Might sound innocent enough to some of you, but believe me, it will only lead to trouble.

And I actually had a conversation once with a person who had gone back to their desk after they were fired because after talking to their leader they didn't realize they had actually just been fired. Yep, that happens.

LET THEM GO

It's hard. You want them to stay. You can't believe they are leaving. I totally get it. But when a senior leader gives you their notice—Let. Them. Go. I promise if you don't, you'll regret it later. Two things will happen if you talk them into staying:

They will ultimately leave anyway.

They will become a less valuable leader because they don't want to be there.

They were going to leave. I get it, it's hard to accept. You take it personally. After everything you did for them, this is how they thank you? You're pissed. But keeping them isn't going to change any of that. You'll think about it almost every day: "I can't believe they almost quit me." And they'll be thinking every day, "I probably should have left."

And for anyone who thinks you need to performance manage a senior-level executive with some formal document … I have good news. You don't.

You sign up for a lot of things when you become a senior executive, and one of them is the fact that a single decision could get you fired. One conversation could get you fired. One board meeting could get you fired.

You wanted the big job, so get over it. You're not getting ninety days to improve your performance. If you're lucky, you got ninety minutes to say some goodbyes.

But that's unlikely.

CHAPTER EIGHT

YOU CAN'T TEACH SOMEONE TO BE A GOOD LEADER

Stop trying. Not being a good leader doesn't mean someone is a bad person. It doesn't necessarily mean they need to be fired or they're worthless to your organization. But if someone who isn't a natural leader is in a leadership role at your company, it does mean you'll never create the type of culture you're hopefully working hard to achieve.

Leadership is something you either have or you don't.

It's easy to find out if you have a bad leader in place. If you don't have the data to pull exit interview feedback or turnover by department, give it the smell test. We did it all the time in retail. At one point in my career, I was in an interim role where I was responsible for 1,100 retail stores in forty-seven states. I could tell within five minutes of being in a store if it had good leadership. If it did, it "smelled" good. If it didn't, it "smelled" bad. I am guessing that all leaders reading this right now are thinking about a department or function they have that doesn't smell right. It's the leader.

THREE MISTAKES YOUR LEADERS NEED TO AVOID MAKING:

Don't let relationships trump performance.

Don't let tenure trump performance (what they did five years ago doesn't matter anymore).

Don't let performance trump behavior (*how* you get the results is just as important).

I can think of dozens of examples throughout my career where a store or a department wasn't hitting its objectives and the turnover was high. We switched out the leader, and two things happened: turnover went way up in the short term and went way down after that—and they started hitting their goals. Think about the Los Angeles Lakers NBA team before Phil Jackson got there. They had Kobe. They had Shaq. You know what they didn't have? A good leader. They switched the coach and, well, the rest is history. They won five titles while he was the coach. A dynasty was built. Before, they had most of the right players but the wrong leader.

I'll offer one of my secrets to assessing talent. Whenever you want to assess whether or not a person you're interviewing will be a good leader, take them out to eat. Preferably somewhere on the nicer side with a host up front. Then watch them interact with the staff—the host, the waitress, the bus boy. The staff in general. It's about a 99.9 percent match to how they will treat employees at the company. Will it be with respect for what they're doing? Will it be casual? Will it be genuine? More than once, I've changed my mind about a candidate based on how they treated a server.

Trust me, it's accurate.

LEADERSHIP IS SOMETHING YOU EITHER HAVE OR YOU DON'T.

CHAPTER NINE

SWEARING AT WORK— WHO FUCKING CARES?

My dad was a high school English teacher for thirty-four years. When I was old enough to learn this valuable lesson, he told me, "Fuck is the most powerful word in the English language, as long as it is used appropriately."

It was actually one of the most valuable lessons he taught me. I've spent my career trying to prove him right.

One of the things I hated most when I was in human resources was when I walked into a meeting and someone said something like "Oh, HR is here, make sure you don't swear" or "Oh, HR is here. I'm not telling that joke anymore." Or something related to the idea that you have to act differently because someone from HR is there.

How do you act when someone from HR isn't there?

I don't understand leaders who think behaviors, interactions, or events need to change when/if an HR person is present. It's not hard—hire adults and treat them like adults. You have to know your audience, and you have to use some common sense. But if you swear outside of work and it's part of your vocabulary, then why don't you do it when you're at work?

Let's go back to the leader who makes the comment about changing their behavior because someone in HR is present: you need to pick a side. Either you have a culture where things like swearing is acceptable or you don't. But nothing is worse for your organization than leaders who change who they are because of who is present.

I was asked to do a presentation on Zoom for a group of about thirty leaders. The owner of the company was not comfortable with the word "asshole" on one of my slides. We went back and forth for a few minutes, and against my better judgment, I changed the word on the slide (it was changed to "jerk" ... not even close to the same meaning). But the person who asked me to do the presentation was someone I really respected and she worked for the owner, so I didn't want to put her in a tough spot. During the presentation, I said, "The word I use in the book is different, but I wanted to be respectful this morning." At the end of my presentation, we did breakout groups, and one of the leaders asked me what word I used in the book. I said "asshole." Everyone in the breakout group said, "Oh yeah, that's way better … you should have used that."

Exactly. I promised myself I would never do that again.

Be who you are. As an individual and as a company.

Be real. People see fake. Fake sucks. Genuine leaders create a culture high-performing people want to be part of and build teams high-potential people want to be on. The path to a bad culture is filled with fake leaders.

They need to stop the act and lighten the fuck up.

NOTHING IS WORSE FOR YOUR ORGANIZATION THAN LEADERS WHO CHANGE WHO THEY ARE BECAUSE OF WHO IS PRESENT.

GREAT LEADERS MAKE SURE MONDAY MORNING DOESN'T SUCK

CHAPTER TEN

ARE YOUR HR LEADERS ANY GOOD?

I learned a lot from my mentor, Dan. Like most mentor-mentee relationships, it ended. I miss talking to him. I miss learning from him. He's the best HR leader I've ever known. I've tried hard to teach others the way he taught me.

Really good HR leaders are typically very polarizing personalities. About half the company thinks they're amazing, and the other half … well, does not think they are amazing. Half the people thought Dan was an incredible HR mind. The other half thought he was crazy. Both were true, depending on who was doing the thinking.

He told me once, "Eric, you'll know you're doing your job well as an HR leader if you walk into a room with six people and:

- "Two of them will be excited to see you and say, 'Awesome, Eric is here.'

- "Two of them will be indifferent and say, 'Hey, Eric' or don't acknowledge you at all.

- "And two of them will say, 'Oh shit, Eric is here.'

"But the important thing to gauge is that the next time you walk into the same room with the same six people, you get the same six reactions—but the reactions have changed from person to person."

I didn't really understand what he meant at the time. I was probably twenty-seven or twenty-eight years old. Damn, he was so right. A lot of HR leaders get one reaction when they walk into a room. Indifference.

Does your HR leader evoke emotion in people? Are they a polarizing personality? Are there people in the room who are glad to see them and some who aren't?

REALLY GOOD HR LEADERS ARE TYPICALLY VERY POLARIZING PERSONALITIES.

Or do you have Toby from the TV show *The Office*? I miss that show (if you're not familiar with *The Office*, get on Peacock and binge-watch it. It won't disappoint). The show was a weekly reminder that a lot of HR talent in a lot of companies is a Toby. Toby was a joke. He was a person who showed up every day and added absolutely no value. He knew it too. That was the worst part.

I remember an exchange I once had with an SVP at a Fortune 100 company. I was telling him how his team felt about some of his behavior—basically telling him they thought he was a bad leader—and he did not like it one bit. He said, "I have never had an HR person talk to me like this before." I said, "Well, I'm always glad to be first, but you should have heard this twenty years ago." He sat back in his chair, crossed his arms, and decided I was sarcastic enough that he could like working with me. We went on to have a great professional relationship.

The problem is that too many HR professionals would never say something like that to a leader. Worse yet, they'd never even have the conversation in the first place.

I know I rubbed people the wrong way sometimes when I was in HR. But I'll tell you what—I never drove home feeling like I got disrespected, excluded, criticized, or smile fucked.

Okay, who am I kidding? I had a lot of days where I drove home feeling like I got disrespected, excluded, and criticized. But I never drove home without having had an honest, direct conversation with a leader.

Oh, yeah, smile fuck. Let's talk about that. It's a real thing. One of the greatest terms I've heard in my career, and I got it from the head of HR at a Fortune 100 company.

If you work in human resources, you surely know what that means even if you've never heard the expression before. It's when a leader looks at you, says, "Yeah, thanks for the feedback, that's a great idea," and has absolutely no intention at all of taking your feedback. In fact, they resent it.

Call it like you see it. Don't be a Toby.

Another thing I learned from Dan was the greatest compliment an HR leader will ever get is hearing a business leader repeat something you said to them as if it were their own idea without giving you any credit.

That's right. Absolutely no credit to you is the biggest credit ever. Sounds strange, but it is true. If you're a CEO or executive reading this book or if you're in a position where you have someone in HR as a dedicated support to you, ask yourself the following question: when was the last time your ideas, approach, direction, decision, investment, response, or reaction was driven or influenced by your HR leader? You may not have realized it at the time, but think about it. If you can honestly answer "never," make a change. Soon.

When I talk about how an organization should leverage its HR leadership, I usually ask leaders to consider the following: If you assume a key decision for your company will be made at a business dinner, is your HR leader sitting at the table for appetizers, or do they join you for dessert? Even better, do they ride in the car with you on your way to the restaurant?

If you don't have your HR leader sitting at the table during the discussions and you only include them in the "we've made the decision and need you to execute it" phase, you either have the wrong HR leader or the wrong value placed on the role.

Or possibly both.

DON'T SMILE FUCK.

CHAPTER ELEVEN

LIVING ON THE EDGE
OF TERMINATION

If you're a really good leader, it's going to happen. Maybe not today, maybe not tomorrow, but you will get fired. Someday. I hope. I think losing your job is the most wonderfully terrible experience that everyone should go through at least once in their life.

I was lucky enough to get fired twice. It's a gift. Embrace it.

Of course, it's an incredibly humbling thing, losing your job. The range of emotions you experience from moment to moment are second only to ones you felt in middle school—the only other most wonderfully terrible experience everyone should go through at least once. The life of an executive has changed, evolved really. The days of going to the same office every day for forty years, retiring with a full pension, and having the company throw you a huge retirement party where they give you a watch are long gone. And they aren't coming back. Ever.

A good executive reaches a point in their career where every time they get called to their boss's office, they question one of two possibilities: "Am I about to get promoted or about to get fired?" It's almost that black and white. And it should be. It's hard being an executive. It's hard leading people. It's hard creating a culture that high performers want to be a part of. And it's really hard getting year-over-year increases in a highly competitive world.

Thanks, Amazon.

So why does the word "fired" have such a negative connotation? If you're in the workforce long enough, there's a good chance you'll be dealing with getting terminated, and being an executive won't shelter you from the possibility—it might even make it more likely. Steve Jobs got fired. So did Walt Disney, J. K. Rowling, and Michael Bloomberg. Oprah Winfrey was told she was "not fit for television." Jack Ma wasn't even hired at Pizza Hut.

What do these leaders have in common? They didn't give up. The highest batting average in the history of professional baseball, a sport that's over 150 years old, is .366, held by Ty Cobb. That means that for every ten times he tried, he got a hit less than four—and he is the all-time record holder in a sport that started in 1869. Think about that. Every ten times he tried, he was successful less than four. What if executives thought that way? For every ten opportunities my company gives me, I'll be a hall of famer if I am successful .366 times. It's something to think about. If you lived it, I bet you'd take more risks. I bet you'd accept failure. And I bet you'd swing for the fences more often than playing it safe by laying a bunt.

Stop being embarrassed to tell people you were fired. I'm not suggesting that you get excited about it, but accept it, learn from it, grow from it, and change from it.

Get humbled.

We all need to be humbled a few times in our lives. Especially as adults, some of us more than others. And whether we like it or not, we all have the same last sentence to our story. It most certainly ends. What we do when we're writing the pages is entirely up to us. Some will lay a bunt, some will get on first base, and some will break the all-time record by being right more than they were wrong—like four out of ten times—and end up in the Hall of Fame.

LOSING YOUR JOB IS THE MOST WONDER-FULLY TERRIBLE EXPERIENCE THAT EVERYONE SHOULD GO THROUGH AT LEAST ONCE IN THEIR LIFE.

CHAPTER TWELVE

START WITH THE LEADERS

I had just started my consulting business and was spending an afternoon working on the book. I got a call from a former peer, a good friend of mine, who was frustrated and wanted to talk. We spent about thirty minutes on the phone, and as soon as we hung up, I wrote this chapter.

He joined a company about three months earlier that was in the enviable position of growing despite being in the middle of a global pandemic. He was a director of HR, and his boss tasked him with implementing a leadership development program that they would use with every high-potential employee. They had a culture that was unique and attractive and were about to hire almost one hundred new employees to support their growth. They knew they had some opportunities to improve their culture, but for the most part they were happy with it ... as he described it to me, "Overall, we are in good shape, but there are a couple leaders I have questions about."

When he started to work on this project, his first question to his boss (the head of HR) was if they could spend time assessing the leaders in the company to make sure they had the right team to implement a program like this.

The response from his boss was about what he expected: "That's not what we need to focus on right now ... we need to get this leadership development program implemented. We can get to that later."

It's really about what came first: the chicken or the egg.

The chicken is LEAD: focusing on the leaders and making sure you have the right people to do something like introduce a new program focused on high-potential employees, a program that is dependent on a certain culture and style of leader to provide the support.

The egg is the project/program that you want to build.

The president of the company and the head of HR were aligned on needing this new program. That's a great start. But this company had almost forty people-leaders who knew nothing about the new program, more importantly, didn't understand the "why," and, even more importantly, thought they would have a say in it.

So … he started building the program. He did focus groups, talked to existing leaders, incorporated ideas from other companies, and did a bunch of awesome work that turned into a really cool two-day highly interactive leadership development program.

Then the company decided to introduce it to the leaders.

During the focus groups, he discovered a huge red flag. One of the new employees mentioned that they had not talked to their leader their first week. And no, the leader wasn't on vacation but literally had not checked in, had not scheduled a meeting, had not taken them to lunch, had not had a conversation with their new employee their entire first week.

He talked to his boss and used that as another reason to do a leadership assessment exercise. His concern about "a couple leaders I have questions about" was just validated. He wasn't using the focus groups to catch people doing things wrong, but it was instant validation that the company had some leaders who didn't understand what being a leader means. Let's be honest. If you have someone leading a team who doesn't make the experience of a new hire their top priority, and if you have to actually tell someone who leads people that they should probably spend time with a new hire during their first week, then … yes, you already said it in your head. That person doesn't understand what being a leader means. You can't teach that. They don't get it, *and* you'll never successfully create a culture that high performers want to be a part of in a company that has someone leading people who doesn't spend time with them their first week. You just won't.

When the new program was introduced to the leaders, it was met with mostly positive response.

Some of the usual questions you'd expect, but it wasn't positioned with enough of the "why." And, unfortunately, it became an "HR initiative" that "HR is introducing," which is much different than "We are [insert company name]. And this is how *we* as a *team* are going to focus on developing future leaders."

It was a few weeks after the new program was introduced. He explained to me that there was a leader who told one of his employees not to go to the two-day program. When the leader was asked why, he explained that "they are already high potential, and I've listed them as high potential, so they don't need any more development. Plus, they are in the middle of an important project, and I need them to finish it instead of sitting in a conference room for two days." My friend was frustrated with this leader, so he decided to talk to his boss about it.

[Pause: This is a pivotal moment in changing culture in your company.]

Remember this bullet from LEAD: support the direction of the company with no hidden agendas.

The head of HR had the absolutely right response: "Well, this is the program that all high-potential employees go through now. It's not optional. This is part of who we are as a company. Why doesn't he want them to go through it?"

The two of them went back and forth and had the conversation you're probably guessing they had.

Now ... what happens next makes all the difference.

Do you override that leader's decision and have the employee attend the program? The correct answer has to be yes. The answer the head of HR ultimately gave was one filled with understandable frustration: "Fine. Whatever. If he doesn't want them to go through it, then they don't have to."

Well, the challenge to build a cool culture that high-performing people would want to be a part of just got harder. When leaders decide which company program they'll support and which ones they won't, it's kind of like when the inmates begin running the asylum.

If a company makes a decision that something like a leadership development program is important, then every leader in the company has to support the new program. It can't be optional.

More importantly for his boss, the head of HR, consider the impact to your team when you allow leaders to decide which programs they're supporting even after someone from your team explains the "why" and is supporting the direction of the company. While it probably wasn't intentional, allowing that leader to opt out was a blow to her direct report (remember, he's relatively new to the organization and still building his brand as an HR leader). How do you think he feels about his relationship with that leader now? He's frustrated because he knows that leader will never listen to him or take him seriously because that leader validated that they can "do whatever they want."

It's hard. It's really hard. Doing an honest assessment of your company's leaders and having the honest conversation about which ones can help you build the cool company you want to build and which ones can't is gut-wrenching at times. It's hard because you have to be decisive and make the tough call on talent.

But it isn't really that hard. You know which leaders are good and which ones aren't. Every company does. Knowing how to move on with the right people and change the bad leaders is something a lot of companies never do.

If you're not sure, you're sure.

When it comes to talent … you're sure most of the time. Whether you do anything about it will make all the difference to your team and culture.

POOR PERFORMING EMPLOYEES DON'T QUIT VOLUNTARILY.

CHAPTER THIRTEEN
A LEADER'S JOB IS SIMPLE

Imagine if every employee you had was high potential and a high performer. Monday morning would be a lot of fun. Why do we let ourselves settle for anything less than that? Hire slow and fire fast. Address the one or lose the nine. Create a culture that high performers want to be part of.

Why is it that some employees get a sick feeling in their stomach on Sunday evening as soon as they start thinking about work? As I explained earlier, I'd argue it's one of three things:

- They are a high performer, and their boss hasn't told them yet.

- They are a low performer, and their boss hasn't told them yet.

- They are stuck in the middle looking for direction, and their boss hasn't given it to them yet.

It's that simple.

Monday morning sucks when you have employees who are not engaged and not capable of doing the jobs they are in.

A fish rots from the head. It always starts at the top.

Don't blame it on the company culture—that's driven by you as a leader. And if you don't feel like you can change the company culture, then it might be time to leave. If the real reason you're not able to build the culture you want is resistance or unwillingness from your CEO, the executive team, your peers, the board of directors, or something that, unfortunately you probably aren't going to be able to influence, then it might be time to take your show on the road.

If there's a chance you can influence it, then you've got to lead. Do your managers know what's expected of them? If I asked them what your company expects of them, could they answer? I'm not talking about obvious stuff like driving sales, increasing shareholder value, and improving year over year. That's a given. I'm talking about what is expected of them *every day* to make sure that Monday morning doesn't suck. I'm talking about LEAD.

A FISH ROTS FROM THE HEAD. IT ALWAYS STARTS AT THE TOP.

LEAD

LEADERSHIP EXPECTATIONS AND DEVELOPMENT

- Create a culture high performers want to be a part of

- Bring energy and enthusiasm to work every day

- Build relationships at all levels of the organization

- Support the direction of the company—no hidden agendas

- Be decisive—make the tough call when it needs to be made

- Manage the performance of your team(s)

- Consistently deliver results

- Help the company grow by developing people

It's a simple list of the things that truly good leaders do. When you implement a tool like LEAD, it becomes a game changer. A turning point if you need one. You'll have clarity on who your good leaders are and confirm which ones aren't helping you create a culture that high performers want to be a part of. Tweak my list so it sounds like something you and your leaders would actually talk to people about or use it exactly as it is written—whatever works best for you.

When you have a consistent set of expectations, it makes performance-related conversations easy. Take a minute and think about someone on your team who isn't performing at the level you'd like them to. Now think about sitting across from them, reading through these expectations, and pointing out where they fall short.

It's not personal; it's based on the expectations we have of you as a leader. Pretty simple. Are you like some leaders and avoid having these conversations? You need to be able to do that because your high performers deserve more from you.

But what about how hard it is to manage multiple generations in the workplace? And what about the notion that millennials are ruining the workplace as we know it?

I think that's the dumbest conversation taking place in companies right now. Really? Having multiple generations in the workplace is the reason your culture sucks? It isn't the fact that you have bad leaders who don't know how to create a culture high-performing people want to be a part of? That you haven't accepted that bad leaders will never create a good culture? And that everyone at your company knows Monday morning sucks?

I truly believe that there are three things people want when they go to work: a cool place, with cool projects, and cool people. I don't care if you're twenty-two starting your first job after college or sixty-two on the home stretch toward retirement.

We all want a cool place (a culture we like), with cool projects (engaging and rewarding work), and cool people (no assholes).

Do me a favor. Tomorrow, ask someone in your company if they think it's a cool place, with cool projects, and cool people. If they say yes, congratulations. If they say no, maybe you can get some great feedback and be the driving force for change.

That is, only if you're really willing to sign up for what being a strong leader means and live on the edge of termination.

IF YOU THINK YOU NEED TO DO AN ENGAGEMENT SURVEY, ASK YOURSELF WHY?

If your company feels like they need to do an employee engagement survey to "get a pulse" on the organization, then I'd argue you already have the answer. I worked at a company once where we didn't do an engagement survey the first two years we were building it.

We didn't need to. We had just consolidated four companies into one. We had just consolidated four corporate HQs across four different states into one. We had just hired more than 150 people from multiple departments at all levels in less than six months to run the company.

We were voted one of the Top Five Best Places to Work our first year—and we'd only been around for eight months. We had 0 percent voluntary turnover our first year. We didn't need to do an engagement survey because we knew we were building an incredible place to work. Our leaders were focused on creating a culture high performers wanted to be a part of. That's it. No survey needed.

We made sure Monday morning didn't suck.

CHAPTER FOURTEEN

HAVE TO HAVE VS.
NICE TO HAVE

I was the director of HR for the store's division of a Fortune 100 company that was sold. We were sold to two … hmm, how should I put it … *aggressive* venture capital firms. It was a good experience to go through. I learned what was one of the best lessons I ever learned in my career: there is a big difference between "have to have" and "nice to have" in the workplace.

When you stop and think about what your company truly needs to operate, it is always a lot less than you think. A lot less.

The first time we met one of the venture capital firms that bought us, we had a meeting at our corporate office in California. The leader from the VC firm who was running the meeting walked in and said, "We are going to get started soon, but I made an observation when I walked into your office. There is some woman in the lobby watering your plants. If she's watering your plants, that means they're real, and if they're real, that means they cost money."

He went on to explain how shocked he was that we would pay money for plants when we were performing so poorly and had lost so much revenue over the past few years.

The plants were gone by the end of that meeting. Literally. He made sure of it.

At the time I thought, *Wow, I guess we're not in Kansas anymore.* Then about a month later, the president of the company and I were having a beer, and we looked at each other and said, "Hmm, why *did* we still have live plants?"

We thought we had cut so much cost from the business there couldn't possibly be that much left to cut. Now it was simply time to execute. The VC firm came in and cut hundreds of thousands in costs.

That's when I realized there was a big difference between have to have and nice to have.

Think about it …

It's nice to have recruiters, but you don't have to; you can outsource that.

It's nice to have an office for your executives, but you don't have to.

It's nice to have free pop (yes, "pop" not "soda"—I'm from Minnesota), but you don't have to.

It's nice to have coffee in the break room, but you don't have to (coffee is for closers anyway. Please watch the movie *Glengarry Glen Ross* if you don't get the reference).

That doesn't mean that making some of the hard cultural decisions won't have any impact on engagement, but if you're in a position where you need to save money, there's no choice. Companies step over dollars looking for dimes every day and don't even realize it.

You have to remember—nobody works for you because you have live plants in the lobby. And if they do, then they don't get what you're trying to accomplish.

They work for you because you have three things: a cool place, with cool projects, and cool people. We covered it earlier—a great culture with engaging work and great leaders.

Hopefully, the people you hire come to work for you because of the leaders you have and the culture they create each day. When I worked at that tech company with the cool culture, we spent almost $100,000 a year on Red Bull. And guess what? In the areas where we had good leaders, the free Red Bull was awesome and appreciated. And in the areas where we had bad leaders, low morale, and high turnover, the Red Bull was abused because people thought, "I hate this place, so I'm going to take advantage of it."

That's the way it works. Bad leaders = bad culture.

Remember Chapter Six? It's my favorite one in the book.

PEOPLE WANT THREE THINGS WHEN THEY GO TO WORK: A COOL PLACE WITH COOL PROJECTS AND COOL PEOPLE.

CHAPTER FIFTEEN

LESSON #3 BECOMES RULE #3

Holy shit. It worked. I can't believe it.

Those were the words ringing in my head when Lesson #3 became Rule #3. I was the chief talent officer at a retail organization and had spent the previous six months building out a new corporate headquarters. We hired more than 150 people in less than six months. We focused on cultural fit. We focused on energy and enthusiasm. We focused on each candidate's ability and interest in helping us create a cool place with cool projects and cool people. But most importantly, we focused on Lesson #3.

I interviewed every candidate that would lead people: manager, director, vice president, C-suite. And in every interview, I brought two sheets of paper: LEAD (leadership expectations) and the three lessons I've learned along the way.

LEAD

LEADERSHIP EXPECTATIONS AND DEVELOPMENT

- Create a culture high performers want to be a part of

- Bring energy and enthusiasm to work every day

- Build relationships at all levels of the organization

- Support the direction of the company—no hidden agendas

- Be decisive—make the tough call when it needs to be made

- Manage the performance of your team(s)

- Consistently deliver results

- Help the company grow by developing people

The three lessons I've learned along the way:

- **Lesson #1:** It's okay to have fun at work.

- **Lesson #2:** Poor performing employees don't quit voluntarily.

- **Lesson #3:** Assholes are assholes. They don't change.

I literally spent every interview I conducted (more than 150 in six months) talking about these two things—leadership expectations and the three lessons. That's all I talked about. I figured the hiring managers could do the boring stuff like making sure the candidate could actually do the job.

We hired a general counsel who fit everything we wanted and ended up being a great guy to work with—a truly great leader and even better person. He had been working at the company for about six months when I got a text from him. I saved it because it might be the best text message I've ever received:

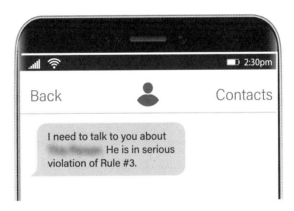

I knew what he wanted to talk to me about—a leader who was not living the values of the company and was creating a lot of angst in the office. But when I read his text, I honestly had no idea what he meant when he said this leader was in violation of Rule #3. The dots just didn't connect. I had been calling them lessons.

I walked into his office and said, "Hey, I want to hear the feedback, but what the hell is Rule #3?"

His response: "What do you mean? It's your rule! You told me when you interviewed me that we wouldn't let assholes work here. You talked about three things and the last one was about the type of leaders you promised we'd have here. Eric, he's not an asshole. He's a major asshole, and you need to get rid of him. I quit my job and came here because you told me I wouldn't have to work with leaders like that."

I had called them lessons, but he wrote down "rules" during our interview. And I realized in that moment that *rules* was *way* better.

It was honestly like twenty-five years of working my ass off, trying to be the anti-HR HR leader, coaching leaders who didn't want to hear what I had to say, feeling like I wasn't making progress, and being fired twice was validated in one simple text.

It works. Trust me. Drawing a line in the sand that you will not let bad leaders work in your company is powerful. The most powerful thing I've ever seen.

I remember being kind of speechless … like, you mean people actually listened to me and were aligned around the commitment that we wouldn't let bad leaders work here? And better yet, people are self-policing now?

How amazing is that?

So, I walked back to my office, and ordered 150 coffee mugs that had one thing written on them:

Then we did a desk drop and every employee who worked at HQ got one. Nothing else. No explanation, no card telling them why they got the mug. Just the mug sitting on their desk when they came into work. Oh, and yes, it was a Monday morning—the Monday morning after we fired the only leader working there who was in serious violation of Rule #3.

Then it just sort of took care of itself. Hallway conversations: "Hey, what is Rule #3?" "Oh, you don't know about Rule #3? Let me tell you …"

And we built an amazing place to work. We had fun. We addressed the one so we didn't lose the nine … and we had a cool place with cool projects and cool people. Monday morning didn't suck.

"No assholes." It's fun to say and gets a laugh when I'm telling the story or giving a speech. Not every company will be comfortable with that kind of language; if not, pick something else that works for you. But you have to have your version of Rule #3. You have to. Because bad leaders will destroy everything else you do right.

Of everything I've learned in my entire career across multiple organizations in multiple industries, I can tell you this is the most powerful rule your company needs to enforce. Get it right, enforce Rule #3, and you might stand a chance of creating a company where Monday morning doesn't suck.

When I think about how it all played out—starting with a simple text I got from the general counsel—it was the single greatest moment of my career.

RULE #3: ASSHOLES ARE ASSHOLES. THEY DON'T CHANGE.

CHAPTER SIXTEEN

IF IT'S BROKE, FIX IT

Then one day everything changed. I was the chief talent officer at the same retail organization when my boss asked me to step into the role of interim chief sales officer (head of stores, responsible for more than one thousand locations in forty-seven states and over five thousand employees).

What? But I'm in HR.

So one day I am leading the HR function as chief talent officer, and the next day I take over for a leader who had been in sales his entire career.

And it wasn't a popular choice with our seasoned sales leaders.

"What? He's an HR guy."

"What does he know about sales?"

You get the picture.

I wasn't a seasoned sales executive. And that was the best part of the interim role—I was about to lead a sales organization and had very little sales experience.

Remember earlier in the book when I said, "I'm an HR guy that really doesn't know that much about HR"? Yeah. Same thing. Exactly the same thing.

I had four area vice presidents of sales that reported to me. They had twenty-three regional sales directors who reported to them. They had 120 district sales managers who reported to them. And 1,100 store managers who reported to them.

Sorry, tell me again why I needed to be a seasoned sales executive? Seems like we had about 1,247 of them.

Any guesses on what I did in the interim role? Read Chapters One through Fifteen again.

The first thing I did was say thank you … a lot. I went on a self-proclaimed "world tour," visiting more than one hundred locations in my first ninety days. I shook a lot of hands, gave a lot of high fives, and thanked the employees who actually got things done: our store managers and sales consultants.

And I apologized a lot.

I was in a store in Tennessee that had everything working against it. The internet didn't work. Lights were broken. Fixtures were missing. The carpet looked worse than the one in my college dorm room. The sign out front was old, dirty, and outdated. Cords hung from the wall, and extension cords ran everywhere to keep the displays lit. They had two parking spaces for the entire store and didn't have enough product to sell. They had submitted several "tickets" to our HQ team to get all this fixed and had been waiting more than two months with no response, and somehow this store manager loved working for our company. He was high energy, enthusiastic, and an "I'll just figure out a way to get it done" kind of guy. How is that possible? We treated him terribly. So I told him that.

"I want to apologize for the way this company has treated you. We have treated you like shit. It's embarrassing. You deserve better. Thank you for not giving up on us and for being a great leader. And thank you for what you do every day to help this company grow."

The regional sales director looked at me and said, "I wish I recorded that because I can't believe you said it."

But it was true, and they both knew it. Don't dodge the issue. Don't lie. If you're wrong, own it.

Then things started to get better. I had hours of conversations with leaders at our corporate headquarters and hours of conversations in our stores trying to understand why our current methods weren't working. Why did every store I walked into complain about their Wi-Fi? How and when did we lose our pride? Would you shop at that store? Yeah, neither would I.

I was visible. I hit Diamond Medallion status on Delta airlines by the end of October. For everyone who thinks Diamond Medallion is "cool," it isn't.

You have to be honest. You have to be genuine. And if you say you're going to fix something, you better fix it. And if you can't, then at least explain *why*.

I'll let you in on a little secret. If you are genuine, and if you listen after you ask questions about what isn't working, people will eventually tell you. But it takes time. I asked the same question to almost every employee I met: "What's the worst part about working here?" I met 120 employees in almost forty stores before word was out that I actually wanted to know the answer. So they started telling me. And we started fixing all the stuff that was broken.

If you lead an organization with hourly employees who are expected to represent your brand and can't connect with them in a genuine way that isn't forced or fake, that comes across as authentic, you're going to have a challenge getting people excited about working there. And yes, I see that all the time.

The night before my first day visiting stores as the interim chief sales officer, I started thinking about how to recognize the thousands of employees we had and, more importantly, help everyone understand that we were all part of something pretty special. For some reason I thought about Best Buy and how they called their employees in the stores "blue shirts," which was a badge of honor.

Then I thought about Home Depot and the orange aprons. I knew a few people who had worked there and had heard stories about how proud employees were to wear their apron, especially when they could hang things on it like pins they got for tenure or special achievement.

YOU HAVE TO BE HONEST. YOU HAVE TO BE GENUINE. AND IF YOU SAY YOU'RE GOING TO FIX SOMETHING, YOU BETTER FIX IT.

So, I came up with my version of "blue shirts." Something to define who we were as individuals but, more importantly, who we were as a company. We had a cool corporate headquarters, but without the team in the field, none of it mattered. Everything had to be about our sales consultants, our store/district/regional managers and the regional vice presidents. We needed something that represented the people who got it done, every day. They were the only reason I had a job. During my first two store visits, I was giving a lot of high fives, thanking people for being part of this, and using this new term I had come up with.

I happened to be traveling with my boss, our CEO. After the second store visit, he posted a picture on LinkedIn we had just taken with the store manager, and under the picture, he added a hashtag to the term I was using. I was sitting in the backseat and asked, "Did you just hashtag that?" Yes, he had.

It became the call to action we needed. It did more than I could have imagined … it took off and people started using it. It grew organically across the entire company. It grew quickly because our leaders rallied around it. It wasn't something marketing told us we needed to use when we posted on social media. It wasn't another poster we needed to hang in the break room. It wasn't something leaders told people they had to use. The employees started using it because they *wanted to*.

Almost as powerful as Rule #3.

What's your hashtag? Do you have something the entire company is rallying around? Do you have something that makes your employees proud to be associated with? I mean, genuinely proud to be associated with? Imagine your employees posting things on social media about your company, not because they have to, but because they are truly proud to work there.

Wow, we had that … and it was awesome.

CHAPTER SEVENTEEN

EVERY STORE. EVERY TIME.

Shortly after I was no longer the interim chief sales officer, I was asked to move into the chief administrative officer role for the organization. This new role had responsibility for all functions that made sure our stores could operate every day: talent, training, asset protection, IT, and facilities.

There was a reason this version of the CAO role was created.

We had a big issue at our corporate office—people didn't understand that their job, at the end of the day, was to support our stores. Remember, we were a retail company with more than one thousand locations in forty-seven states and five thousand employees. Our CEO had a great mantra: "There are only two jobs here—one that supports customers directly and one that supports people who support customers directly."

Unfortunately, we had too many people who didn't believe that, didn't like that, or ... who knows. So we changed the name. We no longer had a corporate office, or a corporate HQ, or an ivory tower. We now had the SSC: Store Support Center.

We held a meeting with everyone at the SSC and gave them a challenge. A goal. Actually, more than a goal—an expectation of everyone who worked there: **Every store. Every time.**

What if every time a store called the SSC with an issue, we solved it? What if every time a customer called with a complaint, we addressed it? What if every time a store wasn't set up to maximize their potential, we found a way to fix it? What if every employee who works in one of our stores believed that we had a Store Support Center ready to help them be successful? What if?

Then we introduced another concept: *stewardship*.

You can look up the definition if you want, but here's mine: stewardship is about leaving it better than it was before. In everything you do, every day.

STEWARDSHIP IS ABOUT LEAVING IT BETTER THAN IT WAS BEFORE. IN EVERYTHING YOU DO EVERY DAY.

Is the department you lead better than it was when you took over? Does your company have more people promotable than it did six months ago? Is the customer in a better place than they were when they walked in? Are sales better than they were last year? Did you push in the chairs and throw your garbage away when you left the conference room after your meeting? (Come on, people, it's not that hard to push chairs in when you're leaving a room.)

You get the idea. What if everyone came into work every day with a goal of improving something? That day. Every day. What would that look like in your company? It doesn't matter if you're a retailer or not. If you're a business, then you have customers and you have employees. Are your employees clear on what their role is on behalf of the customer? I think most employees understand what their job is: accounting, marketing, payroll, procurement, recruiting, operations.

But that's their *job*.

Do they understand their role on behalf of your customer? That's different.

It's easy to find out. Just ask them, "What do you do every day on behalf of our customers?" You might be surprised by the answers you get.

CHAPTER EIGHTEEN

CANDIDATE AND EMPLOYEE EXPERIENCE

Does your candidate experience match your employee experience? Meaning, does everything you promise during an interview become reality when that person starts?

Unfortunately, it probably doesn't.

There's an old joke that goes something like this …

A high-potential candidate receives offers from her top two preferred companies. She is torn; she can't decide which one to join. To her surprise, both companies invite her to come spend a day at their offices. She goes to Company A and has a great day. Nice people, nice culture, engaging work; this one's going to be hard to beat. But then she spends a day at Company B. Wow. She is blown away. Nap pods. Free lunch. Free daycare. A corner office. Unbelievably talented and friendly people. The promise of a fast track to the top.

She chooses Company B.

On her first day, she's confused. No nap pods. Lunch was terrible and expensive. No office, just a small cube.

She walks around until she finds a supervisor and asks, "Hey, I was here last week, and it looked way different. The people were friendlier, and there were a bunch of perks that are nowhere in sight."

The supervisor says, "Well, last week you were a recruit. Today you're an employee."

I hope that doesn't hit too close to home. Do you deliver on the interview? It's a valid question. When a candidate leaves, they have an idea in mind of what the job is going to be. There's a reason they will accept if you offer them the job. Will they be glad or disappointed they chose you?

And let's talk about the candidate experience. It's bad. If you've never been in transition, never had to look for a job, then you might not realize it. But ask anyone who's had to find a job in the last ten years about their experience and you'll get an earful. Résumés fall into dark holes. Hiring managers don't call you back. You go to an interview and wait twenty minutes for the hiring manager to show up for the interview only to have them finish the forty-five-minute interview that started twenty minutes late five minutes early. You feel pretty good about an interview and never hear back. I mean, literally never hear anything back.

I once interviewed at a $2B publicly traded company. I was interviewing for a VP of HR job. I never heard from them. I called. They never called back. I called again. They never called back. I called a third time. Still no call back.

Six months after the interview, I got an automated email letting me know I didn't get the job. I once worked with a very senior-level executive (he was the president at a company I worked for) who interviewed for an EVP position at a Fortune 300 company. He had seven interviews, and the last one was a face to face with the CEO.

He never heard back.

Why treat someone this way? You have to remember that a bad candidate experience is just like a bad customer experience. They tell everyone they can about it.

Consider setting an expectation that every candidate who interviews at your company leaves thinking, *Geez, what a great experience, I really hope I get an offer.* And I mean *every* candidate. Even the ones you know almost instantly you wouldn't hire. Why treat them any other way?

Here are two real-world examples that I could not believe were happening at companies I worked for:

1. We had a director of sales who would walk into an interview, sit down, pick up the résumé, rip it in half, and look at the candidate and say, "I don't really care what your résumé says. You have ten minutes to tell me why I should hire you." Then

he would get up and, on his way out the door, tell them, "Not sure, going to have to think about it," and leave.

2.   We had a very senior-level executive—and I mean *very* senior-level—who, when they had decided they weren't going to hire the person, would crumple up their résumé, throw it in the garbage can, and just sit there until the candidate asked if the interview was over. He would then inform them that it was.

You need to treat every candidate with the same level of respect. Every candidate. The ones you hire and the ones you don't. They took time out of their day to interview. They probably had to use a vacation day. Don't they deserve a little respect?

Now, if you're okay with them telling everyone in their network, "I'd never work at that company. I had a terrible interview experience," then keep doing what you're doing.

If not, then fix it. And if you don't know what's going on in interviews at your organization, find out. Then fix what needs to be fixed. Create an interview process that people find awesome. And make sure the process lives up to its promise from day one onward.

One more thing—if you're not interested in someone, don't interview them. I've always been fascinated when leaders or recruiters schedule an interview with someone they don't really want to meet. They've made up their mind based on the résumé that they wouldn't hire the candidate, but they make them come in for what is inevitably a terrible candidate experience.

YOU NEED TO TREAT EVERY CANDIDATE WITH THE SAME LEVEL OF RESPECT. THE ONES YOU HIRE AND THE ONES YOU DON'T.

Once, I had to eliminate the role of a senior-level HR leader because the position was being relocated and he couldn't move. It happens. No fault of his, no performance issue—in fact, he was a high performer—but the company got a new CEO who had new expectations. Unfortunately, I had recruited the HR leader from his previous company after only nine months, and he had only been with us for thirteen months. So his résumé showed two short-term assignments in a row.

I was a reference for him three different times with three different recruiters. I explained the entire situation. I knew these recruiters. I told them his role was eliminated at absolutely no fault of his own. In fact, I'd hire him again if I could.

Three different times, he went to the interview. And each time the recruiter spent the entire interview "trying to understand why you left both jobs after only nine and thirteen months."

Really? I just told you why. If you had an issue with it, then don't interview him. That's okay. He doesn't care. But if there is no good explanation for the issue you have with the candidate, then do yourself (and, more importantly, the candidate) a favor and don't interview them.

The only thing you will do is create a bad experience for the candidate and waste an hour of your time. Or probably forty-five minutes because you were fifteen minutes late.

CHAPTER NINETEEN

THERE ARE ASSHOLES ON ZOOM TOO

I started my consulting firm in January 2020, about sixty days before any of us heard about this thing called COVID-19. Little did anyone know just how real it was, how much it would change our lives, and how the workplace as we knew it would be changed forever.

When I published the first edition of my book, I was invited on a lot of podcasts. I love being a guest on podcasts, and it was an incredibly humbling experience at first (it still is, but especially the first two or three that I did). It seemed like there was one thing people wanted to talk about more than anything else, and that included Chapter Six: "How do you lead people when everyone is working from home? How do you build culture through a monitor?" How do you create a culture high performers want to be a part of without an office?

You build culture with a remote team the same way you did before … by not being an asshole.

I get it. It's a lot easier to have a meeting with everyone sitting around the table. It is more fun to hang out in the break room and play a game with your team during lunch (yes, that's a thing and something great leaders do), and it's easier to performance manage in person. Meh—maybe.

But I truly believe that people (before all this happened) who had an engaged leader, someone who cared about them as much when they weren't at work as when they were and someone they felt truly valued their contributions, have had a somewhat seamless transition to this new world of working from home. The person who did not have an engaged leader, the kind that managed the behavior instead of the results, the leader who didn't take time to get to know their team or take time to let their team get to know them, has probably not had a seamless transition to this new world.

Assholes are assholes. They don't change. Even on Zoom.

Are you really going to use a computer monitor as the excuse to why you can't build a culture high performers want to be a part of? I remember being on a call once where someone shared a question they like to ask managers: "Would you want to be led by you?" What an awesome question for leaders to think about! If everything you did last week, the meetings you ran, the conversations you had, the direction you gave … if someone had treated you the exact same way, would you be looking forward to work on Monday?

Hopefully the answer is yes, but the challenge is that a bad leader doesn't know what good looks like. A bad leader doesn't think about things like culture, engagement, succession planning, development, and unleashing the potential in their high-potential people. And a bad leader hates this new world of working from home because they are wishing they still could walk the halls at 4:30 p.m. on Friday to see who's still in the office and who isn't.

Let me ask you a question. Before this thing called COVID-19 came around, did you ever call or text one of your employees for no other reason than to say thank you or to check in and see how things were going? Did you ever send a text message to a high-potential leader letting them know "how lucky you are to have them on your team"? Did you ever send them a text and ask what their kids' favorite pizza was and then have one delivered to say "thanks for everything you did this week"?

None of those things required your team to be in the office. So why does it matter?

High-potential people want to be left alone but also want to be recognized for their contributions. We've all seen enough survey data by now to know that money is no longer the number one thing that keeps people at your company. In most surveys, it isn't even in the top three.

WOULD YOU WANT TO BE LED BY YOU?

When you have a Zoom call with your team, is it agenda-based or conversation-based? What I mean is, is it a "the call starts, and I have six things on an agenda that I need to check off my list so I can give *my* boss an update" type of call? And, by chance, do you spin it by saying, "Hey, I'm just going to get through this quickly to be respectful of your time"? Which is often code for "I really don't want to talk to you, get to know you, or let you get to know me."

Or … do you ask this question at the beginning of a status: "What can I do to help with the things on your list?" "What do you need from me so you can get everything done that you're working on?" And then, "What's new? How are the kids?" Don't insult your high-potential employees with an agenda. And I have news for you—if you don't know exactly where they are at all times with their work because they aren't giving you regular updates and exceeding your expectations consistently, then they are not a high performer. High-potential employees don't need an agenda. They need a cool place with cool projects and cool people.

For all the pain and frustration that we all experienced during the global pandemic, I do believe something positive and unexpected happened in the workplace. Especially when we are talking about leadership and culture, I truly believe that this "new norm" leveled the playing field like never before. If you happened to be a remote employee in your company before all this, then you are very familiar with the "Sorry, I couldn't hear the question because there were too many people talking" issue on a conference call. The very real and very frustrating "I tried to ask a question three times but nobody could hear me" issue. I've been the remote employee, and it sucked. Bad.

Quick side note—for all of us who had remote employees before a global pandemic, why the hell didn't we use Zoom before so our team(s) could be seen? Damn … I feel like such an idiot.

The good news is that now there are no more excuses. None. You can't hide behind being the one who wasn't in the conference room. You can't hide behind "I'm rolling my eyes every time my boss speaks and mouthing really bad things that she can't see" anymore. And you can't hide behind lacking energy and enthusiasm, not supporting the direction of the company with no hidden agendas, and ignoring the opportunity to build relationships at all levels of the organization.

We all have our cameras on.

And how cool is that? Having our cameras on tells us all a little bit about us. I may not have known if you had a dog before (but a great leader did because they got to know their team on an individual level), but now I do because he just jumped up on your lap. I didn't know you liked to golf, but I see the framed picture of you at Pebble Beach on your wall. Why do you have a guitar in the corner of the room? Oh, I didn't know you played! I mean, seriously … how cool is that? Having our cameras on tells a story. And consider writing it if you haven't yet. What's in your background?

Be who you are.

I had lunch the other day with a good friend who wanted some advice because one of her employees refuses to have her camera on. I'm guessing a lot of people who will read this can relate, as it's certainly not the first time I've had that conversation with someone. I don't get that. To me, "I refuse to have my camera on" is the same thing as "I quit but just haven't given you my notice yet." If you're reading this and are someone who doesn't want to have their camera on, ask yourself why. You had your camera on when you used to go into the office. Real-time video, in fact. So what changed? Nothing. But I'd bet good money the people who refuse to have their camera on are not A players. They are not high performers and don't want to be there.

When I think about times throughout my career where I was working for someone I respected in a culture that high performers wanted to be a part of, I can't imagine not wanting the camera on.

I have an exciting secret to share: poor performing employees don't quit (via Zoom) voluntarily either. The same frustration your high-potential employees had when they had to sit next to an under-performer in cube-land is the same frustration they feel when they have to sit next to someone in the new "Brady Bunch grid" on Zoom. To anyone too young to get the reference, just YouTube the beginning of any Brady Bunch episode and you'll understand—they were way ahead of their time and didn't know it.

I was thinking about the three lessons I've learned along the way, and I thought I'd update them for this chapter:

- **Lesson #1:** It's okay to have fun at work … on Zoom.

- **Lesson #2:** Poor performing employees don't quit voluntarily … on Zoom.

- **Lesson #3:** Assholes are assholes. They don't change … on Zoom.

If you're a new leader or just joined a new company and haven't had the chance to meet your team in person, what a perfect opportunity to do something like GTKM (Get To Know Me). Remember that from Chapter Five? It's a simple and easy exercise that has been incredibly effective in every company I've introduced it to. You don't need to be in the same room to get to know each other. You don't need to be sitting next to someone to learn something new that you didn't know before. And you don't need to be in the office to have fun at work. You don't. I have laughed just as much on a Zoom call as I have in person.

There is an amazing company in Minneapolis called Harbinger Partners. It was founded by Scott Grausnick in 1999, an amazing leader who understands what it takes to build a great culture that high per-formers want to be a part of and a place where Monday morning doesn't suck. Scott is one of my favorite people and one of those CEOs who just "gets it." Harbinger Partners is the only company in Minnesota to win the Best Places to Work award seventeen times! Yes, seventeen.

You know what he's been doing since he started his firm in 1999? Letting people work remotely. You know what Scott isn't? An asshole. It can be done. I promise. But it can't be done if you let bad leaders lead people in your company. A bad leader will never create a good culture because they don't know what it looks like. It's not a priority. It's not something they get excited about.

And it's not something they will ever care about, on Zoom or in person.

CHAPTER TWENTY

MAKE THE LAST DAY AS GOOD AS THE FIRST

Companies spend a lot of time focused on the employee experience and talking about culture, but most companies only focus on the experience for employees who are still working there. What about employees who are leaving? And executives? Do you care what they think? Do you spend time thinking about what they will say about their experience at your company when they leave? Will it be positive? Or will it be like my friend who recently had a bad customer experience at a major retailer … he has enjoyed telling everyone he can how terrible it was and how he'll never shop there again. All because of how he was treated.

Employees do the same thing.

I have an idea. What if your company became the first company ever to win a Best Places to Transition Out of Award or even the Best Place to Get Fired from Award? I know it sounds a little crazy, but I am certain my grandfather would have said, "What the hell is a Best Places to Work Award?"

Why don't companies spend as much time preparing for an executive's exit as they spend on their entrance? It's going to happen. Fight it or embrace it, but there is a "new norm" out there and like it or not, you'll be lucky to get three years out of your most recent new hire. According to a study done by Korn-Ferry, the average tenure for a C-suite executive is under five years. Yahoo had seven CEOs in five years.

I worked with a woman once who told me, "When an executive resigns, they are dead to me." Less than two years after she made that comment, she found herself in transition. Funny thing, too, because as she reached out to all those executives who were "dead to her," none of them felt compelled to call her back.

IT'S GOING TO HAPPEN. EXECUTIVES ARE GOING TO LEAVE YOUR COMPANY.

It's going to happen. Executives are going to leave your company. Sometimes it will be their choice to leave, and sometimes it won't. Either way, they will be gone. Is your exit package as compelling as their offer? If yes, congratulations. If no, why not? It didn't work out. So what? You hired them, and they accepted. You liked them once. You probably even offered them a generous signing bonus to join. So why aren't you offering them a generous transition bonus: severance, outplacement, and a long notice period? It costs money to hire executives, and it costs money to fire executives. Period. There is no difference.

I had coffee with someone recently who told me he sought legal counsel and ultimately sued his former employer because after twenty-five years with the company, he was dismissed without warning, discussion, or respect for what he did while he was there. He went on to say, "I was hurt and angry, but I would have walked away if I had just been treated better and offered some assistance."

The days of companies being able to enter every interview with a perspective of "this executive would be lucky to work for us" are long gone. And some of you reading this still believe that's true. It isn't. Your company is just as lucky to have that executive join as they are to join you. Good executives have options. Great executives have lots of options. Sometimes it works out, and sometimes it doesn't.

My son is a senior in high school. We are starting to talk about college and careers. When I think about the conversations we'll have in a few years, I truly believe there will be a day where kids are saying, "But, Dad, I accepted the job because last year they won the Best Places to Work *and* Get Fired from Award." Why wouldn't I join that company?

CHAPTER TWENTY-ONE

DO WHAT MAKES
YOU HAPPY ...

I was listening to an interview once with Sammy Hagar, legendary rocker and tequila mogul. The interviewer said, "Sammy, every time I interview you, you're always so positive. Always in a good mood. Always excited about what's going on. What's your secret?"

Sammy talked about how he made the decision a long time ago to only do things that make him happy. Sounds simple, but why is it so hard for most of us? He said he doesn't hang around people that he doesn't like. He doesn't work on a project if he isn't excited about it. He makes his decisions every day based on whether or not that decision will make him happy.

I used to have a framed print in my office with those words: "Do What Makes You Happy."

My niece Shannon was blessed to be born with that gene.

I talk to so many people who hate their job. They hate their boss. They hate their position. They hate their company. And when I ask them what they are doing about it, it's usually nothing. It's really true that the only person who can make us happy is the one in the mirror. Thanks to the King of Pop for that one.

At one point in my career, I was the president of a consulting firm that worked with executives who were in transition. Most of the time I was meeting them within a day or two of finding out they lost their job, and sometimes I was meeting them within five minutes of finding out. I'll say it again … it's the most wonderfully terrible experience to go through, and I hope everyone has at least one chance to experience it during their career.

When I think about the hundreds of conversations I had in that position, all with executives who needed to find a new role, there was one thing almost everyone I ever met with would say: "Eric, I just want to look forward to going to work again."

I'm not kidding when I say I talked to hundreds of executives a year, and it was rare to have met someone who "loved their job." Why do we put ourselves through that? If you're not happy, don't like your boss, can't support the direction of the company, hate Sunday night because it comes right before Monday morning, then leave. Start looking. Spend some time on LinkedIn looking through your connections and the companies they work at. Send some emails and meet for coffee. You can make a change.

But almost all the executives I'd meet with, after they just found out the company decided for them that it was time to leave, and for as unhappy as they were the last few years, had not been doing anything about it. I don't really know why it's so hard to do what makes you happy, but for most people, it is. And that's okay, I guess. I don't judge. I really don't. I gave it up a long time ago. I used to do it sometimes, and then I realized I have my own bag filled to the top with stuff to deal with, so no judgment at all.

But ... living with regret is a tough way to go through life.

If you can find the strength to simply acknowledge that the decision you are making is going to make *you* happy, that's all you need to care about.

Period.

Folks are usually about as happy as they make their minds up to be.

—ABRAHAM LINCOLN

IT IS NEVER TOO LATE TO BE WHAT YOU MIGHT HAVE BEEN.
–GEORGE ELIOT

CHAPTER TWENTY-TWO

WRAPPING IT ALL UP

It's just not that complicated. So many leaders make the job a lot harder than it needs to be. It's pretty easy, really. Make sure all your leaders do this:

LEAD

LEADERSHIP EXPECTATIONS AND DEVELOPMENT

- Create a culture high performers want to be a part of
- Bring energy and enthusiasm to work every day
- Build relationships at all levels of the organization
- Support the direction of the company—no hidden agendas
- Be decisive—make the tough call when it needs to be made
- Manage the performance of your team(s)
- Consistently deliver results
- Help the company grow by developing people

And make sure they do it, or at least try to do it, *every single day*.

Then make sure all your leaders understand that their job, regardless of their title, is to make sure Monday morning doesn't suck for the people who work for them.

But ... most importantly do this: establish Rule #3.

If the word "asshole" is too controversial in your organization, then pick something else. But the way your leaders treat your employees is the only competitive advantage you have—and it doesn't matter what product you're selling or what industry you're in.

Do your leaders *lead*? You just need to be honest when you assess them. They either do or they don't. Do they do it every single day? All the time? No exceptions? If yes, congratulations. If no, you need to start making some changes. Start at the top. Start today.

I promise, if you just do this, you'll be successful and your company will perform better than it did before. You'll have engaged employees, and I bet you'll even have fun at work.

You might actually have a place where Monday morning doesn't suck.

And whatever you do, please, please don't let bad leaders work at your company. You know who they are. Everybody in your company knows who they are. Make the changes you need to make. Especially the ones you know you needed to make before you read this book.

I finished my management training program at Target Corporation in March 1995. I was twenty-two years old. The store manager I worked for during my training was the most difficult leader I ever had. People were afraid of him. I was afraid of him. If you were a manager in training, you showed up to work every day thinking he was going to fire you. And he knew that.

And he loved that.

But I graduated from training. As I was leaving, he called me into his office. I was lucky enough to be starting at T-1 (Roseville, Minnesota—the first Target store ever built) on Monday.

I was now officially a manager.

He said, "Eric, I know you think I'm an asshole. And I know everybody in the store thinks I'm an asshole. And I know all the managers in training think I'm an asshole. Well, that's because I am an asshole. Trust me, you have to be an asshole if you're a manager. You can't get people to respect you and do what you want them to do unless you are. If you try to have fun at work or try to get people to like working for you, you'll fail. Good luck with your career at Target."

Then he walked out of his office, and that was it.

On Monday morning, March 6, 1995, I showed up at my new location and began a journey that took me to nine different companies in five different states with seventeen bosses, one position elimination, two firings, and a final chapter in corporate America as the chief administrative officer in a $1.5B organization with over five thousand employees.

I spent twenty-five years grinding away and working my way up the corporate ladder.

And twenty-five years trying to prove him wrong.

WHATEVER YOU DO, PLEASE DON'T LET BAD LEADERS WORK AT YOUR COMPANY.

ACKNOWLEDGMENTS

My wife, Jennifer—Thank you for coming along on this crazy journey with me. Five states, four apartments, three houses, two kids, nine companies, and twenty-three years of love.

My kids, Laurynn and Jack—Thank you for giving me a reason to work hard all those years and for understanding when I missed some of your events along the way.

My parents—Thank you for teaching me the value of hard work and the importance of being a genuinely good person in life.

K. F. C.—Thank you for being the only person who knew about this project, for reading the original rough draft, and for getting this across the finish line.

Jack Daly—Thank you for your support and for making an incredible introduction that accelerated the path forward.

Dan Caspersen—Thank you for teaching me everything I know about what it takes to be in human resources. You were the best mentor I ever had. I miss working with you.

B-Long—Thank you for being the first person (back in 2013) to ask me if I had ever thought about writing a book and for not accepting my answer when I said "no."

Some of the leaders I've known—Thank you for showing me what good looks like.

Some of the leaders I've known—Thank you for inspiring Chapter Six.

My first boss at Target—Thank you for being the original violator of Rule #3 twenty-four years before I even knew there was going to be a Rule #3.

The Fab Four—Thank you Erin Riebe, Jen Sabby, Jim Cram, and Janey Gohl for being the first people to read the rough manuscript and for the feedback you provided.

Dana Fields—Thank you for designing the original graphics for the first version.

Thank you Adam Witty and the Advantage team for everything you did to make this possible.

Rob Cimo—Thank you for giving me the best moment in my entire career by calling Lesson #3 Rule #3 and changing the game forever.

ABOUT THE AUTHOR

Eric Harkins is the president and founder of GKG Search & Consulting, a Minneapolis-based consulting firm that helps organizations get talent, keep talent, and grow talent.

His goal is simple: to help every company he works with make sure Monday morning doesn't suck for their employees. During his twenty-five-year career in corporate America, Eric has held leadership positions ranging from manager to chief talent officer and chief administrative officer.

Eric is a motivational speaker, consultant, executive-coach, and an expert in helping companies create a culture high performers want to be a part of.

If you are interested in booking Eric for a speaking engagement or have needs that his team at GKG can help with, please contact him at:

eric@gkgconsultants.com
www.ericharkins.com